GREAT
SCIENTISTS & INVENTORS

The Wright Brothers

by Emily James

Pebble Plus

raintree

a Capstone company — publishers for children

Raintree is an imprint of Capstone Global Library Limited, a company incorporated in England and Wales having its registered office at 264 Banbury Road, Oxford, OX2 7DY – Registered company number: 6695582

www.raintree.co.uk
myorders@raintree.co.uk

Editorial Credits
Jaclyn Jaycox and Michelle Hasselius, editors; Jennifer Bergstrom, designer; Jo Miller, media researcher; Steve Walker, production specialist

ISBN 978 1 474 7 3445 5 (hardback)
21 20 19 18 17
10 9 8 7 6 5 4 3 2 1

ISBN 978 1 474 7 3449 3 (paperback)
22 21 20 19 18
10 9 8 7 6 5 4 3 2 1

British Library Cataloguing in Publication Data
A full catalogue record for this book is available from the British Library.

Acknowledgements
We would like to thank the following for permission to reproduce photographs: Bridgeman Images: Private Collection/Look and Learn, 7, Private Collection/Peter Newark American Pictures, 19; Glow Images: Science Faction, 21; Library of Congress, 5 (both), 11, 17; Newscom: akg-images, 13, 15; SuperStock: Science and Society, 9; Wikimedia/Library of Congress, cover (both), 1 (both) Design Elements: Shutterstock: aliraspberry, Charts and BG, mangpor2004, Ron and Joe, sumkinn, Yurii Andreichyn

Contents

EARLY YEARS

Inventors Wilbur and Orville

Wright dreamed of flying.

Wilbur was born in 1867.

Orville was born in 1871.

They grew up in Ohio, USA.

Wilbur (left) and Orville Wright as children

Wilbur and Orville's father gave them a toy helicopter. The brothers tried to build their own. They wanted to know more about flying.

7

EARLY WORK

The brothers loved learning about how things worked. In 1892 they opened a bicycle repair shop. They also built and sold bicycles.

the Wright brothers' bicycle shop

Wilbur and Orville started building huge kites and gliders. In 1900 they tested a new glider at Kitty Hawk, North Carolina, USA.

Wilbur and Orville test a glider

Wilbur and Orville wanted
to build better wings for their
flying machines. They studied
birds. Birds use their wings and
the air to get off the ground.

Wilbur pilots a glider in 1902

THE FIRST FLIGHT

The Wright brothers built an aeroplane that could power itself. It had an engine and two propellers. They named the aeroplane the *Flyer*.

the Wright brothers' *Flyer*

Orville flew the *Flyer* in 1903. He flew for 12 seconds and travelled 37 metres (120 feet). It was the first time anyone had flown an aeroplane with an engine.

Flyer's first flight on
17 December 1903

LATER YEARS

Orville and Wilbur continued to make better aeroplanes. In 1909 the brothers opened the Wright Company. They trained pilots and built aeroplanes.

Orville (left) and Wilbur Wright

19

Wilbur Wright died in 1912.

Orville Wright died in 1948.

Today's aeroplanes still use the

Wright brothers' basic ideas.

They proved people can fly.

Wilbur (left) and Orville in 1909

Glossary

glider light aircraft without a motor

helicopter aircraft that can take off and land in a
small space

inventor someone who thinks up and creates
something new

kite object that flies and is made of a light frame that is
covered with paper, plastic or cloth

pilot person who flies an aeroplane

propeller rotating blade that moves an aeroplane through
the air

prove show that something is true

Read more

Planes (What's Inside), David West (Franklin Watts, 2016)

The Wright Brothers (Important Events in History),
Helen Cox Cannons (Raintree, 2016)

The Wright Brothers (Fact Cat), Jane Bingham (Wayland, 2015)

Websites

www.britishpathe.com/video/the-wright-brothers-first-flight
Watch a video of the Wright brothers' first successful
flight in 1903.

www.ducksters.com/biography/wright_brothers.php
Find out fun facts about the Wright brothers.

Comprehension questions

1. What did Orville and Wilbur do when their father gave them a toy helicopter?

2. The Wright brothers tested a new glider in 1900. What is a glider?

3. What was the name of Wilbur and Orville's first aeroplane?

Index